MW00395499

In My English Garden
Beautiful Illustrations For Adults To Color

By Lilt Kids Coloring Books
Illustrated by Petya Kazantseva

COLOR TEST PAGE

COLOR TEST PAGE

"Enjoy free bonus images from some of our best-loved coloring books on the next few pages."

Find our books on Amazon.

MAGIC IN THE GARDEN
The Whimsical Adult Coloring Book

OCEAN FANTASY
Beautiful Mermaid Coloring Book For Adults & Children

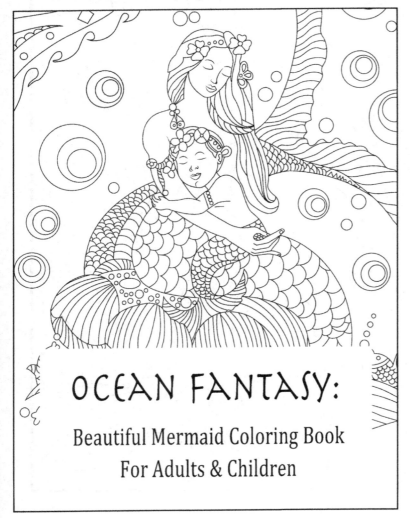

OCEAN FANTASY:

Beautiful Mermaid Coloring Book
For Adults & Children

COLORING INSPIRATIONAL QUOTES
The Uplifting Coloring Book For Adults

Coloring Inspirational Quotes:

The Uplifting Coloring Book For Adults

MAGIC OCEAN ADVERNTURE
Adult Coloring Book

Made in the USA
Coppell, TX
29 June 2020